HOW TO USE THIS BOOK

The first few pages in the book outline the history of the county from the prehistoric period to the recent past. Any words in italics are explained in a helpful glossary at the rear of the book. To find out more about East Lothian's past, go to **www.eastlothian.gov.uk/archaeology**

More than 100 sites are described and located in the subsequent pages. The sites in this book represent just a few of the many archaeological sites in East Lothian. They have been chosen because of their visibility and ease of access. We are grateful to all the landowners who have given their permission for these sites to be included in the book.

At the rear of the book is information on the Scottish Outdoor Access Code, transport in/around the county and other useful information.

We recommend that you use this book in combination with:

Ordnance Survey Explorer Maps 345 and 351
Ordnance Survey Landranger Maps 66 and 67.

PLEASE SCAN THIS QR CODE
INTO YOUR MOBILE DEVICE

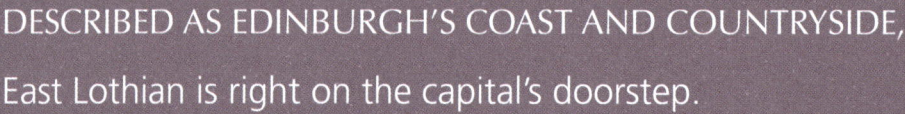

DESCRIBED AS EDINBURGH'S COAST AND COUNTRYSIDE,
East Lothian is right on the capital's doorstep.

CONTENTS

Prehistoric and Roman East Lothian	5
Early Historic to Medieval	6
Medieval and Later Times	9
Defensive Structures	9
Church and State	9
Battlefields	10
Mills and Doocots	10
Harbours	10
Industrial East Lothian	12
Grand Designs - Houses and Policies	12
East Lothian at War	
- World Wars I and II	13
Key to Map Pages	14
Introduction to the Maps	16
MAP 1 ABERLADY AND GULLANE	18
MAP 2 DIRLETON AREA	20
MAP 3 NORTH BERWICK	22
MAP 4 WHITEKIRK AREA	24
MAP 5 ATHELSTANEFORD AREA	26

With excellent road and rail links throughout the county, it's the perfect base from which to explore its archaeological and historic sites. With its beautiful, rolling countryside, distinctive villages and stunning coast, East Lothian has much to offer both the outdoor enthusiast and heritage explorer.

MAP 6	EAST LINTON AND TRAPRAIN	28
MAP 7	DUNBAR	30
MAP 8	DUNBAR SOUTH AND SPOTT	32
MAP 9	BARNS NESS TO OLDHAMSTOCKS	34
MAP 10	MUSSELBURGH	36
MAP 11	PRESTONPANS	38
MAP 12	COCKENZIE, PORT SETON AND TRANENT	40
MAP 13	ORMISTON, PENCAITLAND AND GLADSMUIR	42
MAP 14	HADDINGTON	44
MAP 15	GARVALD AND STENTON	46
MAP 16	HUMBIE AND SALTOUN	48
MAP 17	BOLTON AND GIFFORD	50
MAP 18	WHITEADDER	52

Glossary	54
Scottish Outdoor Access Code	56
Travel in/around East Lothian	60
Useful Links and Information	61

EAST LOTHIAN IS RICH IN BOTH ARCHAEOLOGICAL AND HISTORICAL REMAINS.

With a variety and abundance of resources, East Lothian has attracted settlement since early prehistoric times. In addition to fabulous upstanding remains, the county is also home to a large number of *cropmark* sites, which have been identified through *aerial photography*.

IMAGE: **WHITE CASTLE**
This is a superb example of an *Iron Age hill fort* in the Lammermuirs with panoramic views of Traprain Law, North Berwick Law, and the East Lothian coastline. A clear entrance leads you through the impressive ramparts and onto the gently sloping summit.

PREHISTORIC AND ROMAN EAST LOTHIAN
(8500 BC – AD 400)

East Lothian's rich landscape was first settled by *hunter-gatherers* after the retreat of the ice sheets, around 10,000 years ago. Farming first started in East Lothian in the *Neolithic* and *Bronze Age* periods (4000-800 BC). Standing stones, burial cairns and round houses are examples of some of the sites from this period which can still be seen surviving in the landscape.

The *Iron Age* (800 BC – AD 400) in East Lothian was noticeably different from earlier periods. It was an unsettled time marked by increased building, defence, weaponry, displays of wealth, intensive forest clearance, the adoption of iron technology and the increased visual display of tribal identity.

The main types of site that can be seen in East Lothian from this period are defended settlements and *hill forts*. The landscape around each of these forts would have been extensively cultivated and inhabited by other smaller settlements. The *hill forts* may have been more symbolic centres of spiritual or tribal power rather than purely defensive.

In AD 79 the Romans advanced into Scotland. At this time, East Lothian was inhabited by the *Votadini*, whose capital was believed to be on Traprain Law. In contrast to other areas of Southern Scotland, East Lothian appears to lack Roman military or settlement remains. The exception to this is the Roman fort at Inveresk (Musselburgh), which was established, along with a Roman civilian settlement, during the Antonine period (AD 142-158).

Prehistoric and Roman

EARLY HISTORIC TO MEDIEVAL (AD 400-1550)

Following the withdrawal of the Romans after the early 3rd century AD, East Lothian appears to have descended into a period of instability and change, although there were still close links with the Roman empire.

By the end of the 6th century, the *Votadini* (now known as the *Goddodin*) were increasingly threatened by *Anglian* kingdoms from the south and by the 7th century, southeast Scotland had become part of the *Anglian* kingdom

IMAGE: CASTLE PARK, DUNBAR
This *aerial photograph*, taken in 1989, shows the excavations taking place at Castle Park prior to the construction of the swimming pool. The excavations revealed a long history of fortification, from an *Iron Age promontory fort*, to an *Anglian* fort and settlement, then the medieval castle, and 16th century French fort.

© Crown Copyright: RCAHMS. Licensor www.rcahms.gov.uk

of Northumbria. There are very few upstanding settlement remains of this period in East Lothian, but at Doon Hill the outline of two large halls can be seen. These were originally thought to date from the *Anglian* period but recent research now suggests that they may be of prehistoric date.

Place names in East Lothian reveal the location of both native *British* homesteads and *Anglian* settlements. Dynbaer (Dunbar) and Tref yr neint (Tranent) are examples of *British* strongholds, whereas place names such as Tyninghame, Whittingehame, Morham, Auldhame, Eldbotle, and Bolton denote *Anglian* sites.

It was during this period that Christianity spread into East Lothian, and *Anglian* crosses have been found at Aberlady, Morham and Tyninghame. Sites of worship were being established at this time and in some cases the churches we see today are on the site of these earlier places of worship.

From the 12th century many parish churches were established, but relatively few examples survive in their original form. East Lothian, however, has some fine examples of churches from the later medieval period. *Pilgrimage* also flourished during this period, bringing travellers to East Lothian from as far as Europe, and many sites catered for these holy visitors. There were many other elements which together made up the 'holy landscape', including monasteries, monastic *granges*, holy wells, and springs.

Early Historic to Medieval

IMAGE: **ST MARTIN'S KIRK, HADDINGTON**
A remarkably intact example of an early 12th century church with *buttresses* added during the 13th century. St Martin's Church was originally a chapel belonging to St Mary's Nunnery, Haddington.

MEDIEVAL AND LATER TIMES

Defensive Structures (1100-1800)

The importance of East Lothian and its rich farmland, as well as the proximity of Edinburgh and the border with England, have always made this a landscape which has been fought over. Powerful dynasties and some local families fortified their homes to protect their land or as a symbol of wealth and power. The earliest castles were *mottes*, which were built in the 11th to 12th centuries. Soon these were superseded by stone castles at sites like Tantallon, Dunbar, Dirleton, and Hailes Castle. Numerous tower houses dot the landscape of East Lothian, many of which have been incorporated into later mansions, such as Winton House, Lennoxlove House, and Nunraw House.

Church and State (1550-1800)

From the mid-16th century, there were great changes in Scottish life, both in religion and state politics. It was a turbulent time but also a time when the merchants and *burghers* in the towns were gaining power and influence. Buildings such as the Town House in Dunbar and the Musselburgh Tollbooth represent the places of local justice. The new churches that were built at this time mirror the changes, with plain *Presbyterian* design becoming the norm and older churches being remodelled to the new style.

Medieval and Later Times

Battlefields (800-1745)

East Lothian is home to some of the most important battle sites in Scotland, from the 9th century to the 18th. Each battle was fought over an extensive area, which is now part of the working landscape of East Lothian. In most cases, a battle memorial has been erected to mark the site of the event, and at Athelstaneford an interpretation centre has been created at the *doocot*.

Mills and Doocots (1550-1800)

The landscape of East Lothian is dotted with *doocots* and mills, key elements of the local economy in *pre-industrial* times. Pigeons provided a valuable source of fresh meat, particularly in the winter months. The earliest *doocots* are round dome structures, or 'beehive' *doocots*, while the later form is square in plan with a sloping roof called 'lectern' *doocots*.

Before industrialisation, mills would have been set up to serve a group of farms or a small community. The examples in this book were used to grind cereals harvested from the surrounding fields, using millstones turned by a waterwheel.

Harbours (1500-present)

East Lothian's coast is interspersed with harbours and safe havens which have seen a long history of fishing, trade, and boat building. There are several harbours to visit in the county, all of which have a different story to tell. The coastline is also peppered with wrecks of vessels from throughout the ages, some of which can be seen at low tide.

Medieval and Later Times

IMAGE: **PRESTON MILL**
Preston Mill near East Linton is one of the oldest mechanically working meal mills in Scotland. This mill dates from the 17th century (with later additions) and is cared for by the National Trust for Scotland, with an excellent small visitor centre.

Industrial East Lothian (1800-present)

Although East Lothian is mainly seen as a rural county, it was home to many important and successful industries, which were of massive social and economic importance to the area. Some of these industries started in the medieval period, but the surviving examples tend to date from 1800 onwards, for example, *saltpans*, glass works, *limekilns*, breweries, commercial mills, distilleries, railways, and the great industrial and mining complexes are all products of this period.

Grand Designs - Houses and Policies (1600-1900)

East Lothian has a wealth of beautiful designed landscapes and gardens, created around some of the country's most significant houses. The extensive agricultural estates with their great houses were in decline before the Second World War, hit hard by heavy death duties and the 1930s economic depression. Many grand houses were demolished, such as Smeaton House and Amisfield House, although several still remain. Some of these houses and estates are in private ownership today but there are a number where public access is provided and in some cases, positively encouraged.

IMAGE: LONGNIDDRY BENTS
The beach is almost 2 miles in length, which includes Gosford Bay to the east side, and the rockier Seton Sands to the west. Along the beach are the remains of a wall of concrete *anti-tank blocks* erected during World War II as protection from any attempted German invasion.

East Lothian at War - World Wars I and II

East Lothian played an important role in both the First and Second World Wars in Britain. East Fortune *airship* station was established in 1915-16 as a major element of the strategic network protecting the *British* coastline. Like Drem Airfield and Penston Aerodrome, it also took on a key role during the Second World War, when East Lothian often found itself on the front line. The remains of *anti-tank blocks* and coastal defences are also visible reminders of the impact of the wars on East Lothian.

Medieval and Later Times

HERITAGE EXPLORER
EAST LOTHIAN

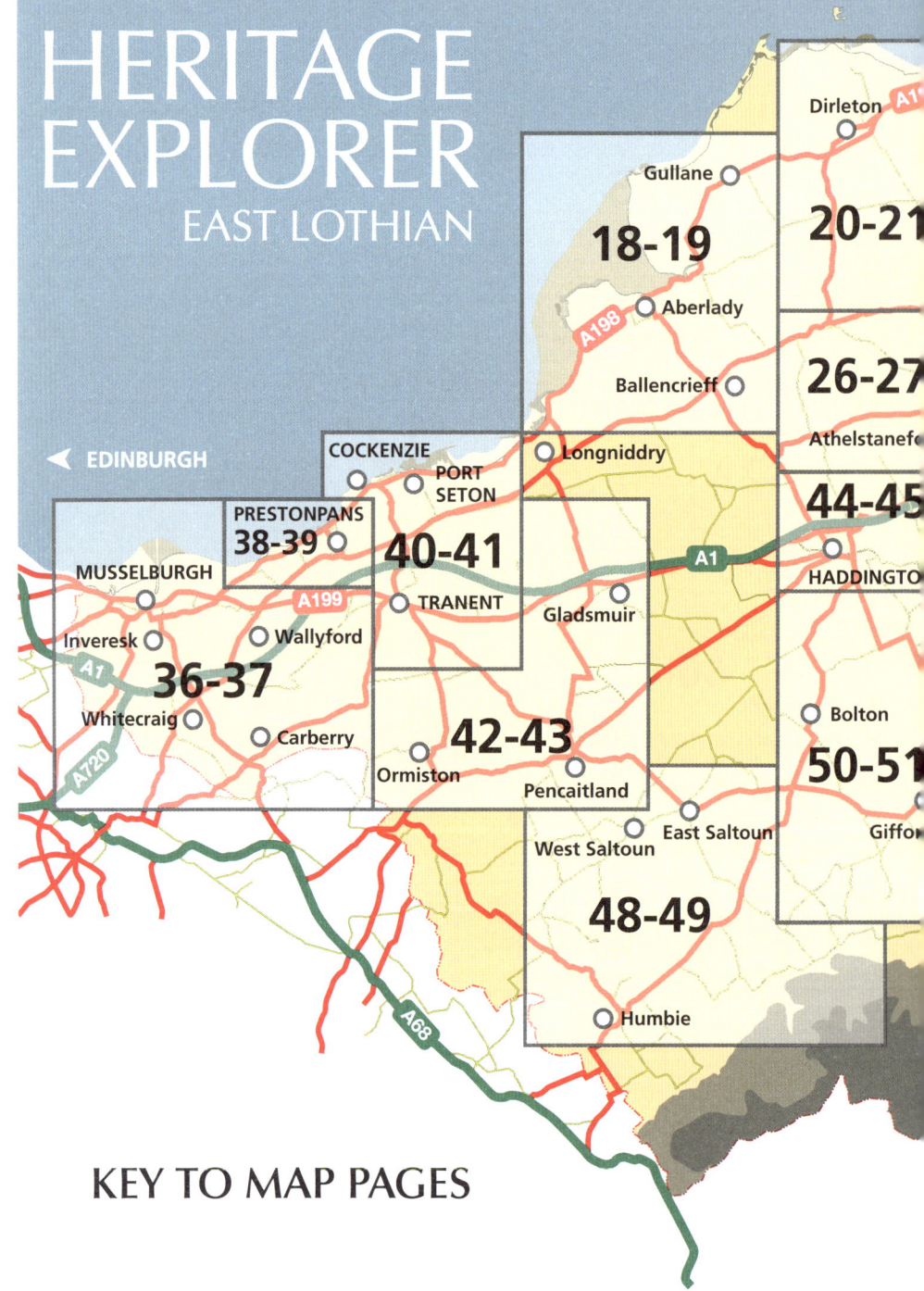

KEY TO MAP PAGES

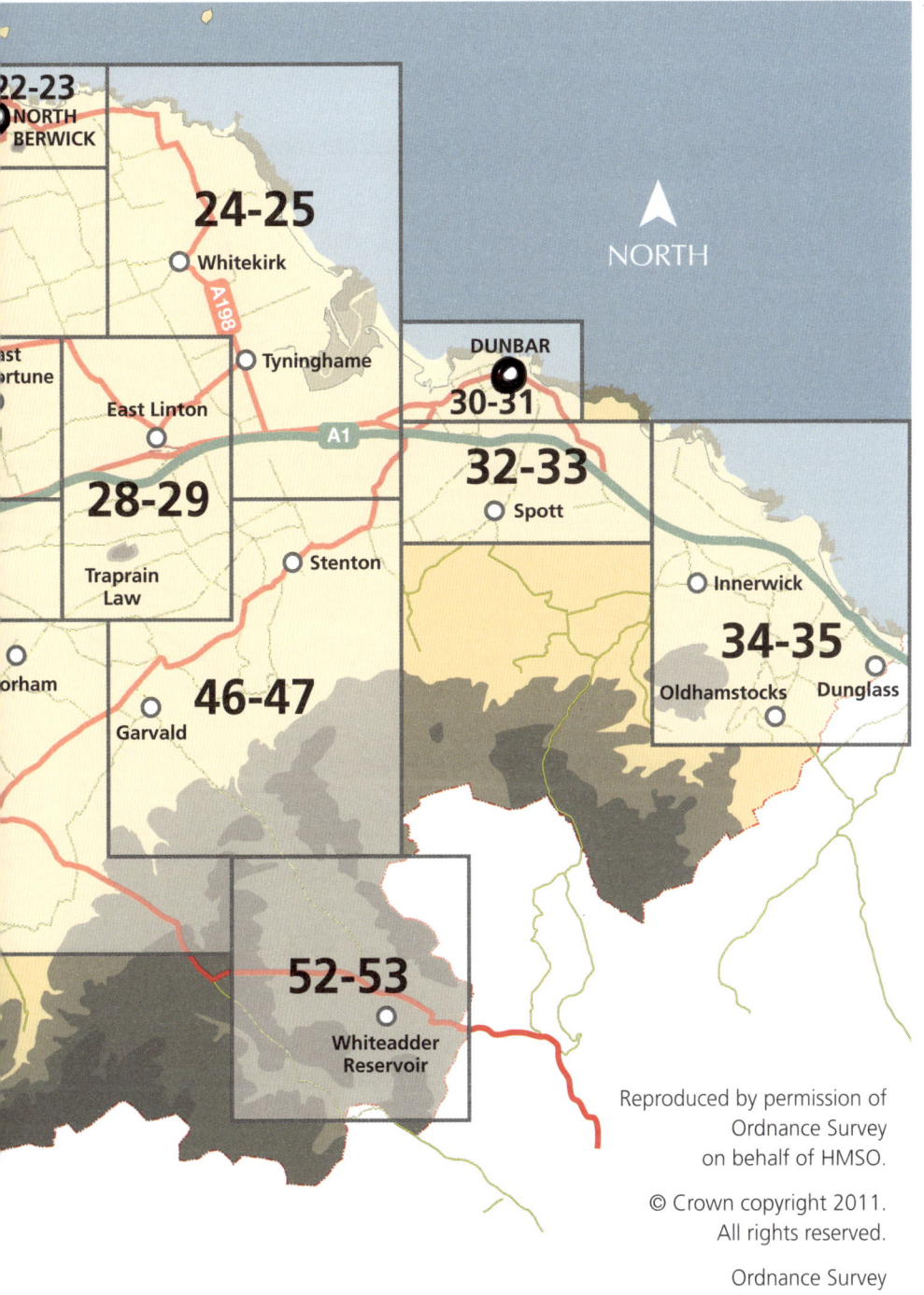

INTRODUCTION TO THE MAPS

OVER 100 SITES ARE DESCRIBED IN THE FOLLOWING PAGES. Each map refers to a different part of the county (see map on pages 14-15) and each site is depicted by both a coloured symbol and a number.

Key

- Major road
- Main road (A road)
- Secondary road (B road)
- Minor road or access road
- Track
- Path
- Railway
- River
- Town, village or buildings
- Woodland
- Higher land (over 250m)
- Rocks
- Sand
- Mudflat
- Archaeological site to visit

Facilities

- Picnic site
- Information
- Parking
- Golf course
- Toilets
- John Muir Way
- Hillfoot Car Trail
- Saltire Car Trail
- Coastal Car Trail
- Walks

TIMELINE
BC 5000 — Mesolithic — 4000 — 3000 — Neolithic — 2000

HERITAGE EXPLORER EAST LOTHIAN | 17

The different symbols indicate the time period to which the site is dated (see Site Themes below). For example, if the site is an *Iron Age hill fort*, it is depicted as a red circle. The colour can also be cross-referenced with the timeline shown below which shows all the different time periods and how they relate to one another.

Further symbols on the maps provide other useful information such as the availability of car parks, picnic sites etc. Small symbols next to each site description identify additional information such as if there are any entrance charges, disabled access etc.

Site Themes

- ○ Prehistoric
- ● Iron Age
- ○ Roman
- ● Early Historic
- ● Medieval Church
- ● Stronghold
- ⊗ Battlefields
- ○ Church and State
- ○ Mills and Doocots
- ○ Harbours
- ✦ Industrial
- ▢ Grand Houses
- ● World Wars I & II

Symbols Key

- 🐕 Keep dogs under proper control
- 👁 Visual access only
- ℹ On site interpretation
- 🕐 Opening hours
- £ Entrance charges
- ✋ No access during shooting season
- ♿ Disabled access
- National Trust for Scotland property
- Historic Scotland property

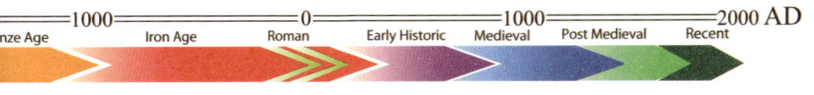

MAP 1 | ABERLADY AND GULLANE

2 LUFFNESS FRIARY (below)
A *Carmelite friary* was founded here in the late 13th century. The walls of the church can be clearly seen and an effigy of a knight in full armour rests within a niche in the church (above). About 100m northeast of the church are the remains of two medieval fishponds. Access via the 'Postman's Walk' path from Aberlady.

5 SALTCOATS CASTLE, GULLANE (above)
The remains of a late 16th century tower house fronted by a massive entrance gatehouse are located within a walled enclosure. At the western side of Gullane, take Saltcoats Road south towards Saltcoats Farmhouse. Bear right before the farm and view the castle from the railway path. Strictly no entry into the castle.

1 **ABERLADY PARISH CHURCH**
A 15th century tower adjoins the 18th century nave of Aberlady Church. An 8th century cross shaft was found here, attesting to the early medieval origins of the site. Evidence suggests that Aberlady had important links with other early Christian centres at Iona and Lindisfarne. To the north of the church a series of interpretation panels illustrates and describes the history of the area.

2 **LUFFNESS FRIARY**
See opposite.

3 **ST ANDREW'S CHURCH, GULLANE**
See below.

3 **ST ANDREW'S CHURCH, GULLANE** (above)
Located at the western end of the High Street, the recently consolidated ruins of St Andrew's Church date from the 12th century. It was abandoned in 1612 after sand dunes threatened to inundate it. The last minister was removed by James VI for smoking tobacco.

4 **KILSPINDIE CASTLE**
Kilspindie Castle is situated in a field to the north of Aberlady Parish Church. All that remains of this 16th century castle are two walls, the base of a door, and an oval gun loop. Archaeological work has identified settlement remains in this field dating to both the Prehistoric and *Anglian* periods, suggesting that Aberlady has had a lengthy and very important history.

5 **SALTCOATS CASTLE, GULLANE**
See opposite.

6 **GOSFORD SANDS**
A series of large reinforced concrete *anti-tank blocks* dating from WWII are set just above the high water mark at the picnic area surrounding Ferny Ness.

7 **GULLANE BAY, MAGGIE'S LOUP**
On the top of the high cliff overlooking the beach below are a number of concrete WWII *anti-tank blocks*.

8 **LUFFNESS LINKS, GULLANE**
A concrete roadblock from WWII sits on the west side of the A198 public road where it takes a sharp bend to the west of Gullane. The block retains the slots for the lifting pole.

MAP 2 | DIRLETON AREA

2 FENTON TOWER, KINGSTON HILL (left)
Fenton Tower was built c.1575, and has recently been beautifully restored. In 1591, King James VI of Scotland / I of England, took refuge here. The tower and immediate grounds are privately owned but can be viewed from the road. For more information go to www.fentontower.co.uk

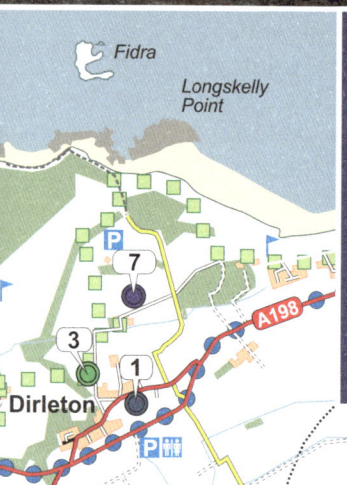

5 BALGONE BARNS WINDMILL (right)
The fabulous remains of a 17th century windmill later converted into a *doocot* in the late 18th century. Located on farm land, there is no access to this site, but it can be seen easily from the road.

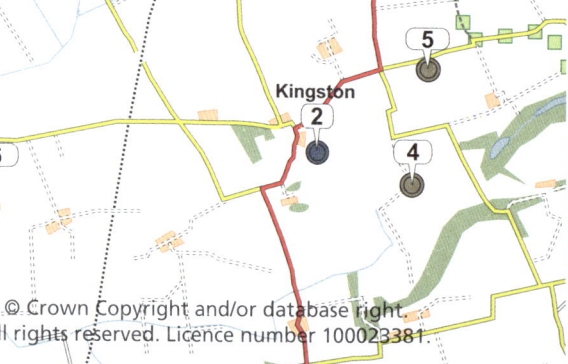

© Crown Copyright and/or database right. All rights reserved. Licence number 100023381.

1 **DIRLETON CASTLE**
See below.

2 **FENTON TOWER, KINGSTON HILL**
See opposite.

3 **DIRLETON PARISH CHURCH**
Dirleton Parish Church was built in 1612 to replace the earlier church at Gullane. There are a number of very interesting gravestones and a small exhibition space at the entrance.

4 **ROCKVILLE FARM DOOCOT**
This cylindrical tower was originally an 18th century windmill, which was later converted into a *doocot*. Located within a working farm steading, there is no access into the *doocot*.

5 **BALGONE BARNS WINDMILL**
See opposite.

6 **DREM AIRFIELD**
RAF Drem started life in 1916 as a home defence landing ground and in 1939 it became the home to Spitfires. It was from here that the first action in the air during WWII took place over the Firth of Forth. Many airfield buildings survive, including the battle command building. The shops at Fenton Barns Retail and Leisure Village are accommodated in buildings once used by the staff of the airfield, one of which was the cinema.

7 **DIRLETON RADAR STATION**
The radar station at Dirleton is one of a handful of Ground Control Radar complexes that have survived down to the present day. The radar station has been converted into a private house and, therefore, there is no access into the building or its immediate grounds. The radar station can be seen easily from the road down to Yellowcraig.

1 **DIRLETON CASTLE** (below)
Dirleton Castle is one of the oldest surviving castles in Scotland, and is also one of the most magnificent. Originally late 13th century in date, the castle was added to in the 14th and 15th centuries. There are vaulted kitchens, grand halls, and pit prisons. The 16th century beehive dovecot is also definitely worth a visit, as are the historic gardens surrounding the castle.

MAP 3 | NORTH BERWICK

1 NORTH BERWICK LAW (above)
A 60 minute walk takes you up through the ramparts of this impressive *Iron Age hill fort* and past the remains of *Bronze Age* hut circles. Built into the northern side of the summit of North Berwick Law are the remains of a WWII observation post, and nearby can be seen the remains of a Napoleonic signalling station. There are fantastic views from the top to North Berwick below and to the Bass Rock, Fidra, the Forth, and Fife.

4 OLD PARISH CHURCH, NORTH BERWICK (right)
Set just behind the High Street and on the edge of the Lodge Grounds are the roofless remains of the Old Parish Church. Originally dedicated in 1659, it is a lovely church to visit and the graveyard has numerous interesting gravestones.

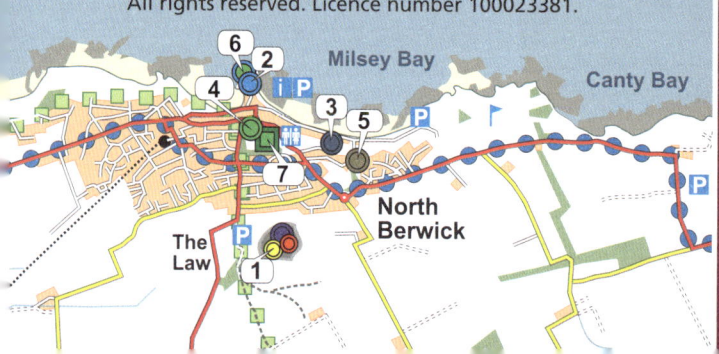

© Crown Copyright and/or database right. All rights reserved. Licence number 100023381.

1 **NORTH BERWICK LAW**
See opposite.

2 **ST ANDREW'S OLD CHURCH, NORTH BERWICK**
The remains of the 12th–16th century church are located on what is now a grassy coastal promontory next to the harbour. The intact whitewashed 16th century porch serves as a small interpretation centre, while the foundations of the remainder of the church can be seen.

3 **CASTLE HILL, NORTH BERWICK**
The remains of a medieval *motte* are found at Castle Hill, North Berwick on the eastern edge of the town. Traces of earthen banking on the summit of the hill indicate the remains of structures.

4 **OLD PARISH CHURCH, NORTH BERWICK**
See opposite and below.

5 **MILLS OF KINTREATH, THE GLEN, NORTH BERWICK**
The remains of three ruined mills can be found in the lovely leafy surroundings of the glen. They belonged originally to North Berwick Priory and are believed to date back to the 14th century. Follow the path along the burn from either Dunbar Road or Tantallon Terrace.

6 **NORTH BERWICK HARBOUR**
The first harbour at North Berwick is mentioned in the 12th century, but what is there now, dates from the late 17th century. Historical sources indicate that pilgrims would stop and rest here before continuing their journey by boat over to Fife and St Andrews. Interpretation boards are sited at the church next to the Seabird Centre.

7 **THE LODGE GROUNDS**
The Lodge and Lodge Grounds are located in the centre of North Berwick at the southern end of Quality Street. The Lodge (in private residential ownership) is a white, harled residence and town house which belonged to the Dalrymples and predominately dates to the 18th century. The Lodge Grounds include the recently restored Edwardian gardens and early Victorian parkland. The grounds and gardens are open to the public.

MAP 4 | WHITEKIRK AREA

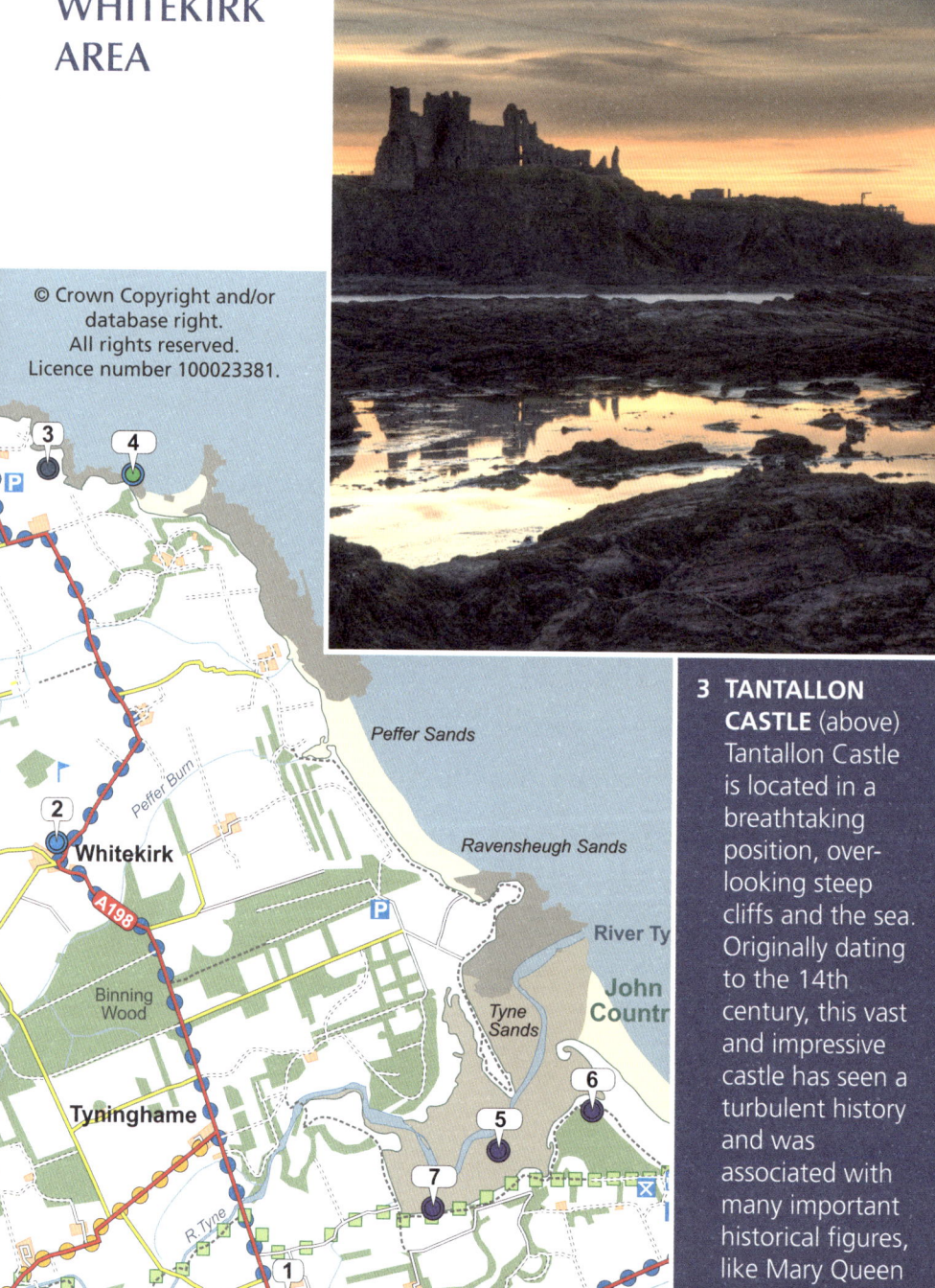

© Crown Copyright and/or database right. All rights reserved. Licence number 100023381.

3 TANTALLON CASTLE (above) Tantallon Castle is located in a breathtaking position, overlooking steep cliffs and the sea. Originally dating to the 14th century, this vast and impressive castle has seen a turbulent history and was associated with many important historical figures, like Mary Queen of Scots.

1 KIRKLANDHILL STANDING STONE
This prehistoric standing stone is located in a field about 300m south west of Kirklandhill steading and is over 3m high. There is no access to the stone but it is easy to see from the A198 road. 👁

2 WHITEKIRK PARISH CHURCH
Whitekirk Church dates from the 15th century but parts were remodelled in the 19th and early 20th centuries. Historically, Whitekirk is very important, and a church has occupied this location since the 12th century. It was a significant stop on *pilgrimage* routes and a nearby well was believed to have special healing properties. 🕐 ℹ

3 TANTALLON CASTLE
See opposite. 🐕 ♿ ℹ 🎁 £ 🕐

4 SEACLIFF HARBOUR
See below. 🐕

5 HEDDERWICK SANDS, BELHAVEN BAY
At low tide in Hedderwick Bay, dozens of wooden posts can be seen protruding through the estuary sands. These are the remains of anti-glider defences from WWII.

6 HEDDERWICK HILL PLANTATION, BELHAVEN BAY
Just off the track in the trees, a brick and concrete WWII building lies behind the sand dunes. Take the path from the John Muir Country Park car park along the front of the Hedderwick plantation for approximately 1km. Concrete shooting range butts lie approximately 60m to the south east. Immediately to the north of the brick and concrete building, traces of zig-zag WWII trenches can be made out in the grass-covered dunes.

7 HEDDERWICK HILL, BELHAVEN BAY
An impressive double row of WWII *anti-tank blocks* extends along the coast edge, next to the footpath.

4 SEACLIFF HARBOUR (above)
This small rectangular harbour cut out of the rock was constructed by the Laidlay family in 1890. It is believed to be the smallest harbour in Britain.

MAP 5 | ATHELSTANEFORD AREA

6 BATTLE OF ATHELSTANEFORD, c. 815–832
Between 815 and 832, a battle took place near Athelstaneford between the Scots and the Northumbrian *Angles* under King Athelstan. The English were defeated and their leader killed. A white X-shaped cloud formation in the blue sky is said to have appeared during the battle, and afterwards became the *Saltire*. The 16th century *doocot* (above) in Athelstaneford (site number **7**) houses an interpretation centre for the Battle of Athelstaneford.

8 EAST FORTUNE AIRFIELD, THE MUSEUM OF FLIGHT (below)
East Fortune *airship* station was established in 1915-16. It was a major fighter base in the 2nd World War and is now part of the Museum of Flight, with many hangars and buildings open to the public. The 2-storey control tower block with flat concrete roof and steel framed octagonal control chamber is a landmark for the area. The Museum aviation collections include aircraft, engines, rockets, photographs, a reference library, archives, models, flying clothing, instruments, and propellers. For more information go to www.nms.ac.uk

1 THE CHESTERS, DREM
See below.

2 KAE HEUGHS, GARLETON HILLS
Situated at the east end of the Garleton Hills right of way, this fort originally may have had four ramparts. It has been partly quarried away, but traces of the interior hut circles can still be seen. The fort is often grazed by livestock and is best seen from the right of way path.

3 SEATON LAW
An important large fort lies on the summit of Seaton Law on the Garleton Hills right of way path. Four ditches can be seen, the innermost of which encloses the sides of a round-cornered rectangular area.

4 BARNES CASTLE, GARLETON HILLS
The ruins of an unusual late medieval castle are to be found along the Garleton Hills right of way. John Seton of Barnes began the construction of the castle in the late 16th century, but he died in 1594, with only the vaulted ground floor complete within an external wall with corner towers. This castle is on the site of a medieval monastic *grange* associated with Haddington Nunnery. Strictly no access to the interior of the vaults as it is used for agricultural storage.

5 GARLETON CASTLE
Built in the 16th century for the Seton family, on land once owned by the Lindsays, Garleton Castle once comprised three blocks enclosed by a curtain wall with gun loops. The castle is on private land and therefore, access is not permitted. It is easily viewed from the road.

6 BATTLE OF ATHELSTANEFORD, c. 815–832
See opposite.

7 ATHELSTANEFORD DOOCOT
See opposite.

8 EAST FORTUNE AIRFIELD, THE MUSEUM OF FLIGHT
See opposite.

© Crown Copyright: RCAHMS. Licensor www.rcahms.gov.uk

1 THE CHESTERS, DREM (above) Easily accessible, the Chesters is an outstanding example of a *hill fort* with impressive ramparts and ditches. Look for the obvious signs of *Iron Age* round houses within the interior of the fort.

MAP 6 | EAST LINTON AND TRAPRAIN

5 HAILES CASTLE (below)
Built on a rocky outcrop overlooking the River Tyne are the charming remains of one of the oldest castles in Scotland, dating from the late 13th and 14th centuries. Entering through

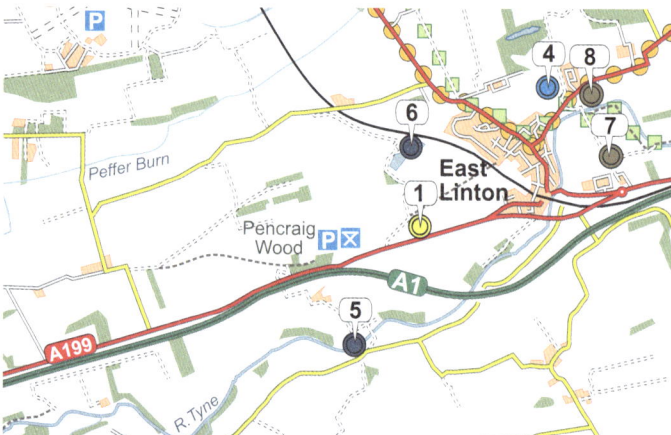

the curtain wall there are two towers, a vaulted kitchen, and a grand hall to explore. It has a fascinating and turbulent history detailed on interpretation panels.

8 PRESTON MILL (above right)
Preston Mill near East Linton is one of the oldest mechanically working meal mills in Scotland. This mill dates from the 17th century (with later additions) and is cared for by the National Trust for Scotland, with an excellent small visitor centre.

1 **PENCRAIG HILL STANDING STONE**
A single prehistoric standing stone sits on a low ridge in the field. There is no access to the stone itself but it can easily be viewed from the right of way towards Markle and from the side of the A199 road.

2 **THE LOTH STONE**
Although not in its original position, this 2m high standing stone can clearly be seen from the path which skirts the western side of Traprain Law.

3 **TRAPRAIN LAW**
Originally called Dumpender Hill, Traprain Law is an isolated hill with a commanding position and a long history of occupation from the *Neolithic* to the medieval period. The site was first fortified in the late *Bronze Age* and became the capital of the indigenous *Votadini* tribe in the *Iron Age*. The famous Traprain treasure of Roman silver was found here last century and can be seen in the National Museums of Scotland in Edinburgh.

4 **PRESTONKIRK PARISH CHURCH, EAST LINTON**
Although what can be seen largely dates from 1770, Prestonkirk Parish Church incorporates the exceptional remains of a 13th century *chancel* and 17th century tower. Recent archaeological work nearby has identified an early Christian graveyard, testifying to the site's lengthy history.

5 **HAILES CASTLE**
See opposite.

6 **MARKLE DESERTED VILLAGE AND LAIRD'S HOUSE**
The remains of a late medieval laird's house and a substantial village can be found to the east of the Markle Fisheries. The Fisheries reserve the right to charge for facilities including parking. The access road is unsuitable for buses. Please respect this is a private business and priority is given to anglers.

7 **PHANTASSIE DOOCOT**
A fantastic example of a 16th century beehive *doocot*, with three rat courses to keep the vermin away from the nesting pigeons. Take the path from either Preston Mill or Phantassie Farm. No access to interior.

8 **PRESTON MILL**
See opposite.

MAP 7 | DUNBAR

6 DUNBAR MERCAT CROSS (above)
A restored 16th century *mercat* cross with carved stone heads is located next to the Dunbar Town House. It was moved to the Town House from its original position. The three human head *skewputts* are believed to have come from the old parish church.

5 DUNBAR TOWN HOUSE (above)
Built in the 16th century, the Town House, or Tollbooth, is the oldest surviving building in Dunbar. This was where the local town council looked after the affairs of the burgh for over 400 years. A stone turnpike staircase takes you up three floors, past the first floor that held prison cells. It houses a small museum and local history centre. Limited disabled access.

© Crown Copyright and/or database right. All rights reserved. Licence number 100023381.

1 **FRIAR'S CROFT, DUNBAR**
   The 15th century tower is all that remains of the medieval *friary* church in Dunbar. It was later converted into a *doocot*.

2 **DUNBAR BATTERY, LAMER ISLAND**
   The fort on Lamer Island was erected in 1781 to protect Dunbar from sudden invasion, particularly by *privateers*. Inside the strong stone wall enclosure are stone platforms for guns and the remains of former buildings. Recent archaeological work tentatively suggests that the fort may be located on the site of an earlier defensive structure.

3 **DUNBAR CASTLE**
   Dunbar Castle has a long and turbulent history. Dating back to the 12th century, the castle was rebuilt in 1494, and was finally ordered to be dismantled by the Scottish parliament in 1567. Although the 19th century harbour and coastal erosion have removed much of this truly important castle, fragmentary remains still survive and it is definitely worthy of a visit. The castle is associated with many important historical figures, including Mary Queen of Scots who was held here after Bothwell kidnapped and later married her. There is no access into the castle and great care must be taken in its vicinity.

4 **DUNBAR PARISH CHURCH**
   This massive red sandstone 19th century church stands on the site of the medieval collegiate church of Dunbar and dominates the Dunbar skyline. The church interior was restored in the 1990's after a fire.

5 **DUNBAR TOWN HOUSE**
   See opposite.

6 **DUNBAR MERCAT CROSS**
   See opposite.

7 **VICTORIA AND CROMWELL HARBOURS, DUNBAR**
   The 19th century Victoria Harbour superseded the much older Cromwell Harbour further to the south east, which is also still in use. Overlooked by Dunbar Castle, Dunbar Battery, and 17th-19th century warehouses, both harbours are well worth a visit.

8 **BELHAVEN BREWERY, DUNBAR**
   Belhaven Brewery was founded in 1719 and carries on a local tradition of brewing dating back to the late 11th century. Guided tours of the historic brewery are available, visit www.belhaven.co.uk for more information. Limited disabled access.

9 **LOCHEND WOOD, DUNBAR**
   All that remains of what was once a fine 17th century mansion and estate are the ruined walls and doorway dated to 1684. Turn down Kellie Road off Spott Road and continue for approximately 500m.

MAP 8 | DUNBAR SOUTH AND SPOTT

7 SPOTT CHURCH (above)
Built around 1800 incorporating a 17th century aisle, Spott Church is in a lovely location on the edge of the village. It is a simple church with an historic interior that includes box pews and an octagonal pulpit. A set of *jougs* attached to the entrance were used to discipline offenders.

2 DOON HILL (below)
Doon Hill is the site of two successive timber halls excavated in the 1960s. At the time it was thought to date from the *Anglian* period, however recent research suggests that the large timber buildings may in fact be prehistoric in date. Follow signs for the site from the A1 and take the track along the southern edge of the field to the car park.

© Crown Copyright: RCAHMS.
Licensor www.rcahms.gov.uk

1 **EASTER BROOMHOUSE STANDING STONE**
Situated in the middle of an arable field is a 2.7m high red sand stone monolith with cup and ring marks on the west face. There is no access to this site but the stone can be clearly seen from the Spott road.

2 **DOON HILL**
See opposite.

3 **ST JOHN'S WELL, SPOTT**
In the field to the west of Spott Church, a medieval well is located within a stone building. Dedicated to St John, there is a local tradition that annual *pilgrimage* was made to the well by the monks of Coldingham Priory. Historical documents also state that this well supplied water to Dunbar during the 18th century. Cross the stone stile beside the old schoolhouse and follow the path to the well.

4 **BATTLE OF DUNBAR I, SPOTT, 1296**
The first Battle of Dunbar was fought between a Scottish force, marching to relieve the besieged Dunbar Castle, and the English under the command of Earl Warren, on April 27th 1296. The English army had just sacked Berwick, and were marching towards Dunbar when they met the Scottish troops. The Scots were routed, and the English went on to occupy most of Scotland. This marked the beginning of the Wars of Independence.

5 **BATTLE OF DUNBAR II, 1650**
The Battle of Dunbar II was fought between Cromwell and the Covenanters under General Lesley on the 3rd of September, 1650. The main action took place between Broxburn and Doon Hill. It was a disastrous defeat for the Scots but one of Cromwell's most important victories. Currently, the best way to experience the site is to either view it from Doon Hill or to visit the battle commemoration stone on the side of the A1087 road into Dunbar.

6 **THE WITCHES' STONE, SPOTT**
This stone marks the site where Marion Lillie, 'The Ringwoodie Witch', was burnt in about 1698. Some say the stone commemorates the last witch burning in Scotland.

7 **SPOTT CHURCH**
See opposite.

MAP 9 | BARNS NESS TO OLDHAMSTOCKS

6 SKATERAW LIMEKILN (above)
This 19th century square plan *limekiln* with 3 draw holes and tunnel overlooks the sea with spectacular views.

1 DUNGLASS COLLEGIATE CHURCH (right)
Situated within the Dunglass estate is the impressive Dunglass Collegiate Church. Built before 1423, the chapel dedicated to St Mary of Dunglass was promoted to Collegiate Church status about 1443. The simple interior is home to a number of grave slabs, some of which are 16th century in date. Despite having been used as a farm building from the 18th century, it is very well preserved.

1 **DUNGLASS COLLEGIATE CHURCH**
See opposite.

2 **'FRENCH CAMP', DUNGLASS**
The so-called 'French Camp' was really an English fort constructed and used during the *Rough Wooing* of 1548-9. The earthworks consist of massive ramparts and deep ditches enclosing a triangular area on the edge of the plateau overlooking Dunglass. An early 18th century gazebo is located on the top of the fort. From Dunglass Collegiate Church walk west along the road through the private estate passing the small lochan on your left. Turn left onto the track marked for Oldhamstocks and after 150m turn left up the hill for about 300m to the fort.

3 **OLDHAMSTOCKS PARISH CHURCH**
Situated in the quiet, rural village of Oldhamstocks, this lovely late-medieval whitewashed parish church was extended with the addition of the Hepburn Aisle in 1581. An early 19th century watch-house is set in the kirkyard wall. An exhibition inside the church describes the history of the building and the village.

4 **SKATERAW HARBOUR**
Skateraw Harbour was one of a number of outlets for the district's limestone quarries. It was built between 1799 and 1825 by two local farmers to ship limestone to ironworks in Devon. Little of the original harbour now survives but some stonework is still visible on the shoreline. The adjacent *limekiln* survives intact.

5 **BARNS NESS LIGHTHOUSE**
(above)
Situated on a beautiful stretch of East Lothian coastline, this lighthouse was constructed in 1901 by the engineer D A Stevenson. The lighthouse is privately owned and there is no access to the interior.

5 **BARNS NESS LIGHTHOUSE**
See left.

6 **SKATERAW LIMEKILN**
See opposite.

MAP 10 | MUSSELBURGH

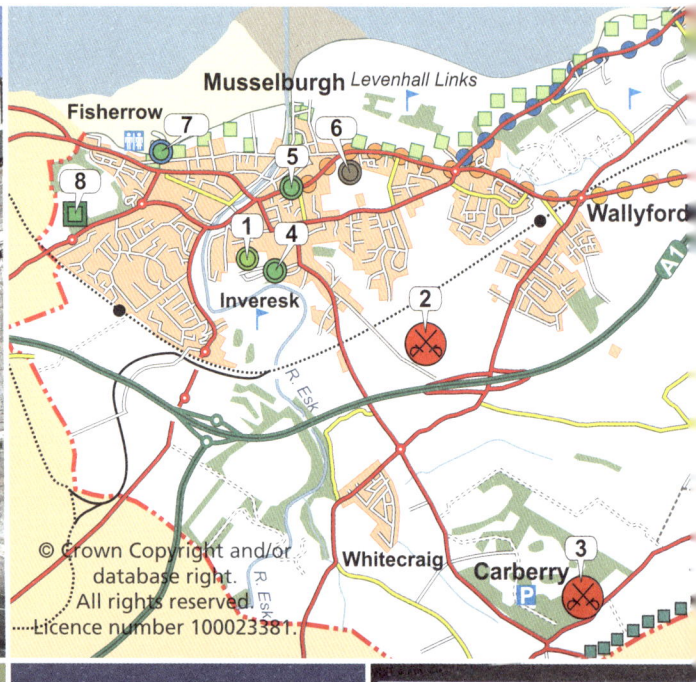

5 MUSSELBURGH TOLLBOOTH
(above) Dominating the High Street, Musselburgh Tollbooth was built c.1590, although the tower may date to the 15th century. There is generally no entry into this building. Musselburgh Museum is located next to the Tollbooth on the High Street.

2 BATTLE OF PINKIE, 1547
The Battle of Pinkie is regarded as one of Britain's most important battle sites. Attempts by the English to link the two kingdoms of England and Scotland, through the marriage of the young Mary Queen of Scots and Prince Edward, the son of Henry VIII, collapsed into open conflict in 1544. The Battle of Pinkie, 1547, was a decisive defeat for the Scots with 10,000 killed. It is an exceptionally important battle site, not just because of the massive losses, but also because it was the first battle in Britain to make use of hand-held firepower in the form of the *arquebus*. There is a battle memorial stone (above) at the eastern end of Crookston Road, along from Inveresk Lodge, National Trust for Scotland.

HERITAGE EXPLORER EAST LOTHIAN | 37

1 INVERESK ROMAN FORT
Strategically located overlooking the mouth of the River Esk, Inveresk Fort was a substantial and extensive Roman Fort built around 140 AD. The fort now lies beneath the current graveyard and little can be seen. A Roman settlement is known to have also existed to the east of the fort under the current village, and Roman field systems and other agricultural remains have been identified to the east and south.

2 BATTLE OF PINKIE, 1547
See opposite.

3 QUEEN MARY'S MOUNT, 1567
Following her marriage to the Earl of Bothwell, Mary Queen of Scots' Protestant Lords rose against her. Their army confronted her at Carberry Hill on the 15th June 1567, where she surrendered and was later imprisoned in Lochleven Castle. The Battle of Carberry Hill was won without a shot being fired. An *Iron Age hill fort* is also located on this hill. Look for the ramparts and dykes as you near the summit.

4 INVERESK PARISH CHURCH
Sited on the location of an earlier church, this very fine classical church was designed by Robert Nisbet of Musselburgh in 1803. It is located on top of a Roman Fort.

5 MUSSELBURGH TOLLBOOTH
See opposite.

6 PINKIE HOUSE DOOCOT, MUSSELBURGH
This is an interesting example of a lectern type *doocot* built c.1600, and it bears the arms of Alexander Seton and Margaret Hay who were married in 1607. Located beside the path that crosses Pinkie recreational ground.

7 FISHERROW HARBOUR, MUSSELBURGH
There has been a harbour at Fisherrow since Roman times but the present busy harbour dates from the 19th century.

8 NEWHAILES HOUSE, MUSSELBURGH
This magnificent 17th and 18th century house and designed landscape is owned and run by the National Trust for Scotland. The house is a superb example of Palladian architecture, which contains amazing examples of early 18th century interiors and collections. There are extensive woodland walks and open parkland, remains of water-gardens and garden buildings such as the shell grotto and classical summerhouse. A shop and café are also available.

MAP 11 | PRESTONPANS

3 PRESTON MERCAT CROSS (top right) Dating to the early 17th century, this is a fine example of a *mercat* cross still in its original location in the medieval village of Preston, Prestonpans. A painted *finial* of a seated unicorn is fitted to the top of the cross.

8 BANKTON HOUSE, PRESTONPANS (bottom right) This striking 17th century mansion with its distinctive orange harl is best known for Colonel James Gardiner who died at the Battle of Prestonpans, 1745. The house has recently been restored, and is clearly visible from either the A1 or from a number of footpaths in the area. Please note that Bankton House is a private residence and therefore there is no access to it or its immediate grounds.

4 NORTHFIELD HOUSE DOOCOT, PRESTONPANS (above) A lovely example of a 16th or 17th century beehive dovecot that has been restored recently by the National Trust for Scotland. Located on the side of the B1361 road, just west of Prestonpans railway station.

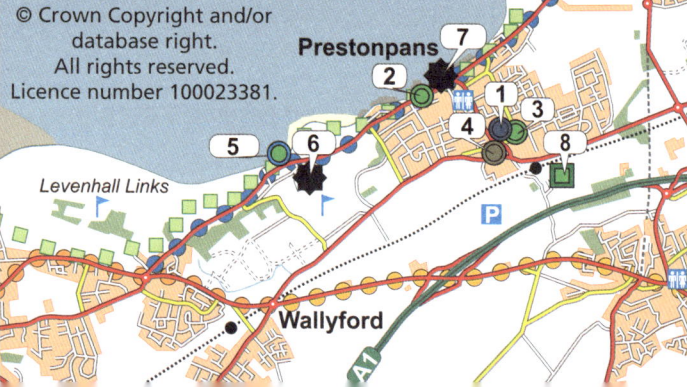

© Crown Copyright and/or database right. All rights reserved. Licence number 100023381.

1 PRESTON TOWER
Preston Tower was built in the 15th century, with a further two storeys added in the 17th century. Now an impressive ruin set within a lovely, small walled garden that is also home to a 17th century *doocot*.

2 PRESTON WEST CHURCHYARD
The graveyard is all that remains of a medieval church that existed here until 1544. There are several very interesting 17th and 18th century tombstones that are worth a visit.

3 PRESTON MERCAT CROSS
See opposite.

4 NORTHFIELD HOUSE DOOCOT, PRESTONPANS
See opposite.

5 MORRISON'S HAVEN, PRESTONGRANGE
Morrison's Haven, a late medieval harbour, is located adjacent to the Prestongrange Industrial Heritage Museum. Although much of the harbour was filled in during the mid-20th century, some of the harbour wall heads can still be seen. In its day, the harbour was a hub of activity and played a crucial role in the development of Prestongrange's glass and pottery industries.

6 PRESTONGRANGE COLLIERY
The site of Prestongrange Industrial Heritage Museum has a long history of coal mining, as well as brick, pottery, glass, and salt manufacture dating back to the 13th century. On site there are the surviving remains of a unique Cornish beam engine, Hoffman kiln, and power house in addition to a visitor centre that interprets the site. Guided tours available. For more information go to www.prestongrange.org

7 PRESTONPANS SALTWORKS
Although the remains of the saltworks in Prestonpans that survive today are 18th century in date, saltmaking first began here in the 12th century. Only the watchtower and outer perimeter wall survive but it is still definitely worth a visit. Accessible via the John Muir Way or down West Seaside, off the High Street.

8 BANKTON HOUSE, PRESTONPANS
See opposite.

MAP 12 | COCKENZIE, PORT SETON AND TRANENT

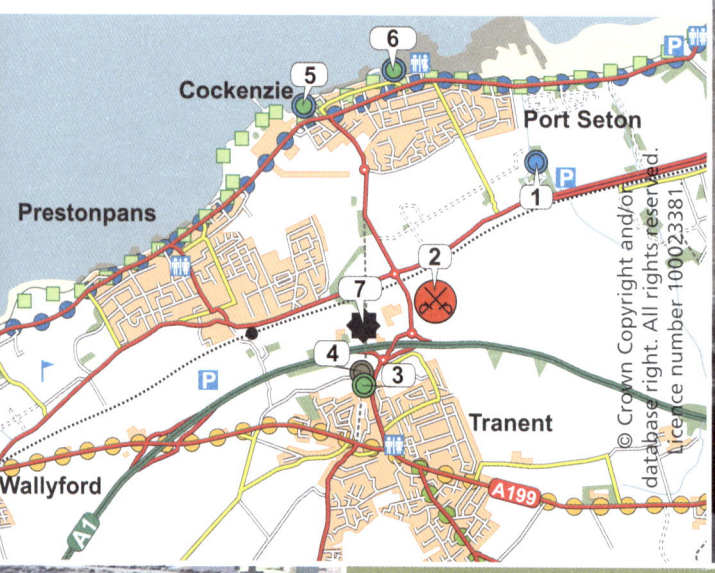

1 SETON COLLEGIATE CHURCH
(above and below)
This is one of the finest surviving collegiate churches in Scotland originally dating to the 13th century. The interior is incredibly beautiful and ornate. This church is within a lovely woodland setting and is an oasis of tranquillity. In the grounds are the remains of what is thought to be priests' houses.

3 TRANENT PARISH CHURCH
Built on the site of an earlier church from the 12th century, the current building dates to 1799. There is an excellent collection of unusual monuments in the graveyard (above) including the ruined mortuary aisle of the Cadells of Cockenzie.

1 SETON COLLEGIATE CHURCH
See opposite.

2 BATTLE OF PRESTONPANS, 1745
The Battle of Prestonpans took place on September 21, 1745 when the Jacobite army under Bonnie Prince Charlie defeated the Royal forces led by Sir John Cope. The best way to experience the site is to either climb up to the top of the viewing mound at Meadowmill or follow the self-guided walk described in the battle leaflet downloadable from www.battleofprestonpans1745.org

3 TRANENT PARISH CHURCH
See opposite.

4 TRANENT DOOCOT
A typical lectern *doocot* with a date on the lintel of 1587. No access to interior.

5 COCKENZIE HARBOUR
See below.

6 PORT SETON HARBOUR
This is a lovely example of an active 19th century fishing harbour, which replaced a 17th century harbour. Located just off the old High Street running between Cockenzie and Port Seton.

7 COCKENZIE WAGGONWAY
The modern path from Tranent to Cockenzie runs along the route of the earliest railway in Scotland dating to 1722. It was used to transport coal from Tranent down to Cockenzie Harbour. Accessible from either The Heugh off Bridge Street, Tranent or Meadowmill Sports Centre.

5 COCKENZIE HARBOUR
(above)
Built originally in the 17th century, this lovely harbour was rebuilt in 1835 incorporating part of the earlier harbour. Located to the immediate east of Cockenzie Power Station.

MAP 13 | ORMISTON, PENCAITLAND AND GLADSMUIR

5 SPILMERSFORD LIMEKILNS (above)
Two impressive *limekilns* of 19th century date sit in woods behind the bus turning circle. The *limekilns* are located on the edge of the village. Take the B6355 south east out of Easter Pencaitland towards East Saltoun.

2 GLADSMUIR OLD PARISH CHURCH (above)
The ruins of a fantastic late 17th century church lie immediately behind the current parish church. This is a really fascinating building with crowstepped gables, birdcage bellcote, and round arched openings. There are several interesting gravestones within the graveyard and lovely open views across the fields towards the coast.

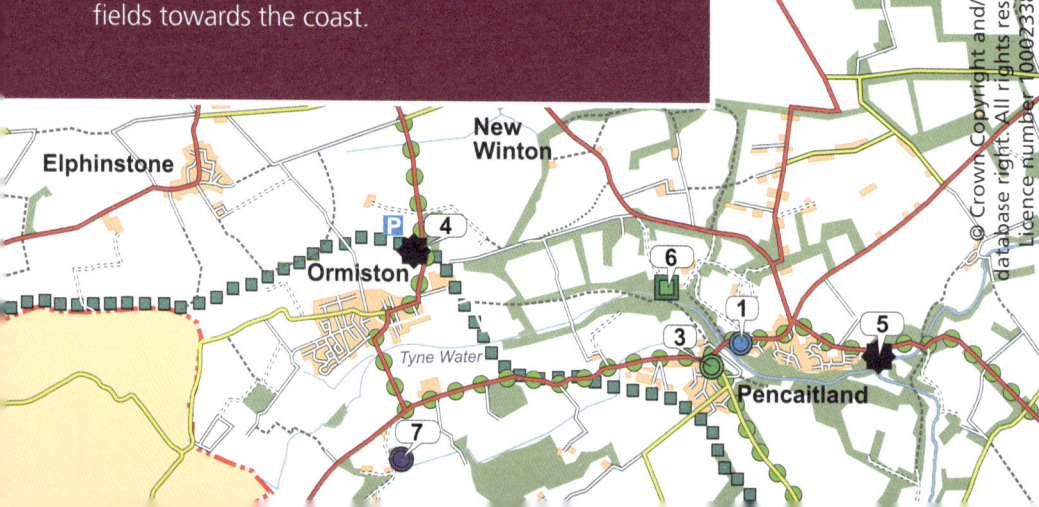

1 PENCAITLAND PARISH CHURCH
Much of this church dates to the 16th century although the aisle projecting north from the *chancel* dates from the end of the 13th century. The graveyard contains a selection of fine gravestones, including ornately carved table-tombs.

2 GLADSMUIR OLD PARISH CHURCH
See opposite.

3 PENCAITLAND MARKET CROSS
The *mercat* cross with a sundial head may date to 1695 when the village became a burgh of barony under Lord Pencaitland.

4 ORMISTON RAILWAY STATION
From 1862 there was a railway line from Edinburgh to Pencaitland. A platform and signal are all that exist of the station at Ormiston but the dismantled railway line now forms part of an interesting walking trail.

5 SPILMERSFORD LIMEKILNS
See opposite.

6 WINTON HOUSE
See below.

7 ORMISTON POLISH CAMP
The remains of a Polish WWII Camp can be found in Ormiston Wood, commemorated with a memorial stone. Following the collapse of Poland in 1939, thousands of Poles arrived in Britain, many of them moving to East Lothian and eventually staying. To find out more about the Polish army in East Lothian go to www.eastlothianatwar.co.uk. From the A6093 Pencaitland to Fordel, take the track south of Ormiston Hall Lodge. Approximately 200m up this track the camp and memorial stone can be found in the woods on the left.

6 WINTON HOUSE (above)
Winton House is one of Scotland's finest stately homes. After the house was burnt down in 1544 by Henry VIII, it was rebuilt in the early 17th century. The house is set within extensive grounds that incorporate estate farms and woodlands. A series of Winton Walks have been created to allow visitors to enjoy the estate. The house and immediate grounds are private but for more information about open days and access to the estate go to www.wintonhouse.co.uk.

MAP 14 | HADDINGTON

4 LADY KITTY'S DOOCOT, HADDINGTON (left)
This charming *doocot* and garden pavilion was built in 1771 as a memorial to Lady Catherine Charteris. The *doocot* is located next to the medieval Nungate Bridge. From Haddington High Street, take Church Street down towards the river.

2 ST MARTIN'S KIRK, HADDINGTON (right)
A remarkably intact example of an early 12th century church with *buttresses* added during the 13th century. St Martin's Church was originally a chapel belonging to St Mary's Nunnery, Haddington.

5 POLDRATE MILL, HADDINGTON (bottom right)
On the site of a medieval mill, the present buildings date to the 18th and 19th century and include a granary and maltings. One of three mills along this stretch of the Tyne, it is the only one still to have an operational water wheel.

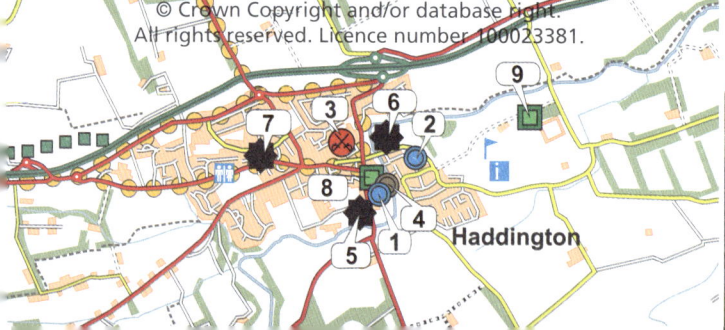

1 ST MARY'S CHURCH, HADDINGTON

St Mary's Church is an incredibly impressive building. It has a history that dates back to the 12th century, however, the majority of what can be seen today is 14th-15th century in date. It is regarded as one of the largest churches built during this period and is comparable to some of the smaller Scottish cathedrals. Much of the church was left roofless after the 1548-9 Siege of Haddington and was extensively restored in the 1970s.

2 ST MARTIN'S KIRK, HADDINGTON

See opposite.

3 SIEGE OF HADDINGTON, 1548-9

The year after the Battle of Pinkie, the English seized Haddington and fortified it. The Scots with their French allies laid siege to the town from 1548 to 1549, when the English were forced to retreat. No visible traces of the fortifications now remain, but St Mary's Church, located just outside the town walls, was used as an artillery tower by the French and sustained much damage during the siege.

4 LADY KITTY'S DOOCOT, HADDINGTON

See opposite.

5 POLDRATE MILL, HADDINGTON

See opposite.

6 BERMALINE MILLS, HADDINGTON

The impressive 19th century mill is on the site of an earlier mill complex, and is one of the oldest industrial sites in continuous use in Scotland.

7 HADDINGTON RAILWAY STATION

This was a terminus at the end of a short branch from Longniddry that closed in the 1950's. The platform and original station house still survive and visitors can walk along the now dismantled railway line to Longniddry. The platform is just off Hospital Road but to get to the station you need to access the railway walk off Alderston Road.

8 HADDINGTON HOUSE AND ST MARY'S PLEASANCE

Dating from the 17th century, Haddington House is one of the oldest surviving buildings in Haddington, with a traditional 17th century style garden behind. There is no access to the interior of the house, but the garden is open to the public. No dogs are allowed in the garden.

9 AMISFIELD PARK

Amisfield Park was largely set out in the 18th century, although it has earlier origins. The house was demolished in 1928, but elements of the parkland can still be seen, such as the Rococo Temple, Gothic Folly, the cascade on the Tyne, and the walled garden which is the second largest in Scotland. A right of way takes you through the park.

MAP 15 | GARVALD AND STENTON

2 ROOD WELL, STENTON (below)
The small circular building enclosing the Well of the Holy Rood dates to the 16th century. The conical stone roof is topped by a flowered *finial* which is said to have come from the church and may date from the 14th century. Located at the eastern edge of the village.

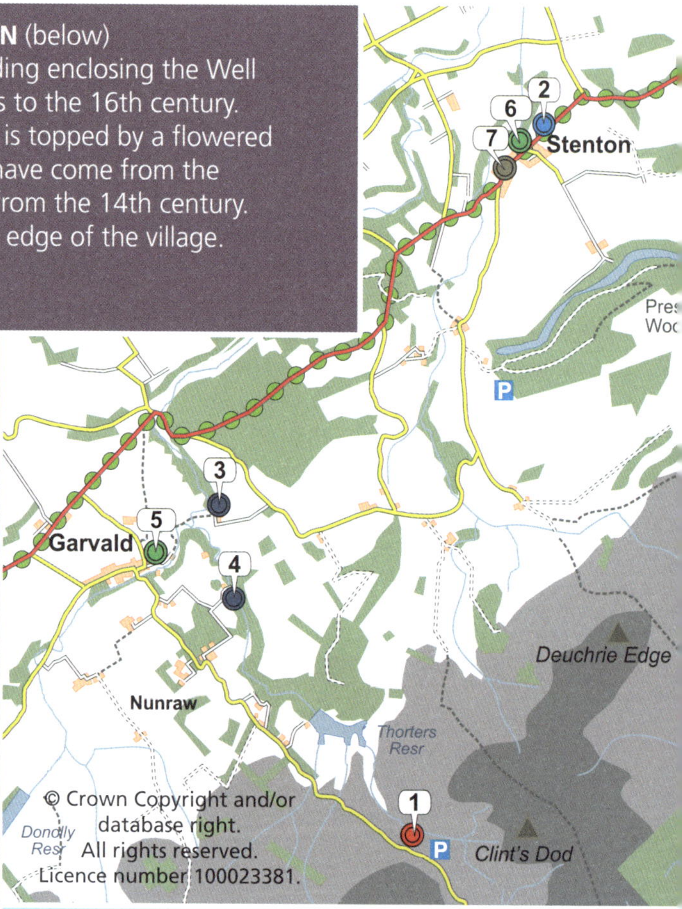

4 NUNRAW HOUSE (right)
Owned by the monks of Sancta Maria Abbey, Nunraw House is a baronial mansion of 1860 incorporating a 15th century tower house. The house and grounds are open to visitors, see www.nunraw.com for details.

1 WHITE CASTLE
See below and page 4.

2 ROOD WELL, STENTON
See opposite.

3 STONEYPATH TOWER
This fabulous 15th century tower house has recently been restored. The tower is in private ownership so there is no access to the interior or immediate grounds. The tower is best approached from the walk along the Papana Water from Garvald.

4 NUNRAW HOUSE
See opposite.

5 GARVALD AND BARA PARISH CHURCH
Located beside the Papana Water, Garvald and Bara Church was completely remodelled in 1829. Part of the 12th century church can be seen in the diamond-shaped stringcourse at the north west corner; the north aisle is of 1677. A pair of iron *jougs* is attached to the west gable near the entrance.

6 STENTON OLD PARISH CHURCH
Considerable remains of the 16th century Old Parish Church, including a prominent tower, survive behind the present parish church. The kirkyard includes a number of 17th and 18th century monuments.

7 STENTON TRON
In the middle of the village is the tron which was used for weighing wool and other merchandise.

1 WHITE CASTLE
(below and page 4)
A reconstruction of White Castle fort by David Simon.

MAP 16 | HUMBIE AND SALTOUN

1. **STOBSHIEL FORT** (above)
Situated close to the road are the substantial remains of an *Iron Age promontory fort* with several stony ramparts and ditches. The triangular interior would have contained several round houses, although none are now readily visible. The site is grazed by stock, please keep dogs under proper control.

4. **SALTOUN CHURCH** (above)
Saltoun Church was built in 1805 on the site of an earlier church, and its fantastic spire is said to have been based on Salisbury Cathedral. Saltoun has been associated with a number of notable families throughout its history, including the Fletcher family.

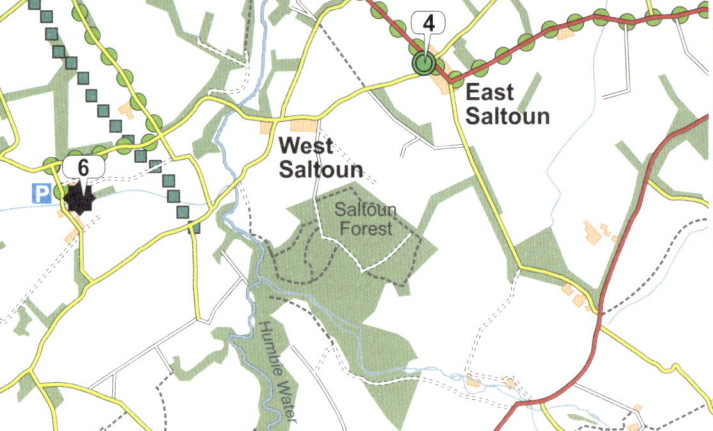

© Crown Copyright and/or database right. All rights reserved. Licence number 100023381.

1. **STOBSHIEL FORT**
See opposite.

2. **WITCHES KNOWE FORT**
The oval fort on the summit of the steep-sided Witches Knowe is slightly smaller than Kidlaw Fort (see right) and lies within the remains of three earth ramparts. Take the track on the east side of Kidlaw Farm and after about 400m take the left hand track. After approximately 600m turn left and follow the track on the northern side of the small reservoir for a further 200m. Take the right hand track up to the fort.

3. **KIDLAW FORT**
On the summit of a hill overlooking Kidlaw Farm are the fabulous remains of two successive *Iron Age* forts (one overlapping the other). The multiple ramparts and ditches represent the second fort. Three stone homesteads were built within the interior of the fort and are believed to date to the 2nd-7th centuries AD. Take the track on the east side of the farm, head south and after 300m skirt round the side of the small reservoir to a track that winds up towards the fort.

4. **SALTOUN CHURCH**
See opposite.

5. **HUMBIE PARISH CHURCH**
See left.

6. **GLENKINCHIE DISTILLERY**
Founded c.1840, this is the only surviving whisky distillery in the Lothians. The distillery is open to visitors and guided tours are available. Go to www.discoveringdistilleries.com for more information.

5 **HUMBIE PARISH CHURCH** (above)
Erected on the site of a pre-*Reformation* church, the present T-plan gothic church was built by James Tod in 1800. This church is in a lovely wooded setting on a bend of the Humbie Water.

MAP 17 | BOLTON AND GIFFORD

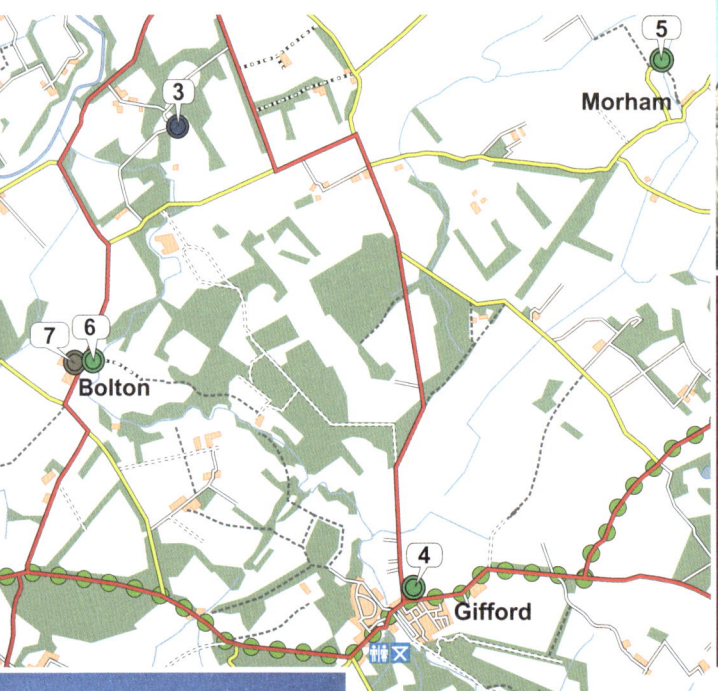

7 UNDER BOLTON FARM DOOCOT (above)
Attached to farm buildings at Bolton, there is a cylindrical 18th century *doocot* surmounted with a fine wooden *glover*. No access to interior.

6 BOLTON PARISH CHURCH (left)
Built in 1809 on the site of an earlier church, Bolton Parish Church has a typical layout for this period in Scotland, of a square church with upper gallery. There is a rare example of a *mort safe* exhibited inside the porch. The brother, mother, and sister of poet Robert Burns are buried in the graveyard, and the remains of Gilbert Burns' house can be seen nearby at Grant's Braes. Limited disabled access.

1 **BLACK CASTLE**
Almost circular in plan, this substantial *Iron Age* fort lies within two ramparts and a ditch. From the side of Newlands Farmhouse, take the track in a south east direction along the side of the burn. After 300m take the track heading north up and around the north side of Black Castle wood and continue eastwards to the fort. There is no access during the shooting season. The site is grazed by stock, please keep dogs under proper control.

2 **GREEN CASTLE**
This *Iron Age* fort rests on the steep right bank of the Newlands Burn and overlooks the reservoir. It has dramatically steep ramparts. Take the track from the Tweedale fisheries. There is no access to the fort during the shooting season. The reservoir is used by fishermen so please take care when walking close to the water.

3 **LENNOXLOVE HOUSE**
Lennoxlove, one of Scotland's most ancient and notable houses, is set within a walled estate of 185 hectares. At its heart is a 15th century castle, incorporated into a 17th century mansion. The famous white cattle of Cadzow, brought across from the Hamilton estates, graze in the fields that line the main drive to the House. Open April to October. Guided tours and group tours available. Go to www.lennoxlove.com for more information.

4 **YESTER CHURCH, GIFFORD**
At the end of Gifford Main Street stands the lime-washed, T-plan church built by James Smith in 1710 as part of the new village of Gifford. The church is set within a circular graveyard and a hearse house was added in the early 19th century. This is a lovely church with an interesting historic interior.

5 **MORHAM PARISH CHURCH**
Morham Church was built in 1724 on the site of an earlier church. A fragment of an early Christian *Anglian* cross shaft was discovered incorporated into the southern wall of the church. A number of interesting gravestones can be found in the graveyard.

6 **BOLTON PARISH CHURCH**
See opposite.

7 **UNDER BOLTON FARM DOOCOT**
See opposite.

MAP 18 | WHITEADDER

3 THE TABLE RINGS, PENSHIEL HILL (below)

A bank and ditch surround a *Bronze Age* barrow burial cairn which sits high on a ridge with impressive panoramic views over Penshiel and Whiteadder reservoir. As you walk south from Penshiel (along the Herring Road) take the rough vehicle track on your right up onto the hill. On the top, bear right and the barrow is approx 90m along and to the right of the track. Please note that this area often contains stock, please keep dogs under proper control. There is restricted access during the shooting season.

6 GAMELSHIEL CASTLE (left)

Set within the striking landscape of the Lammermuir Hills, sits a small ruined castle of 16th century date. Take the track from the fishery car park which heads north and at the burn follow the path up stream for about 500m.

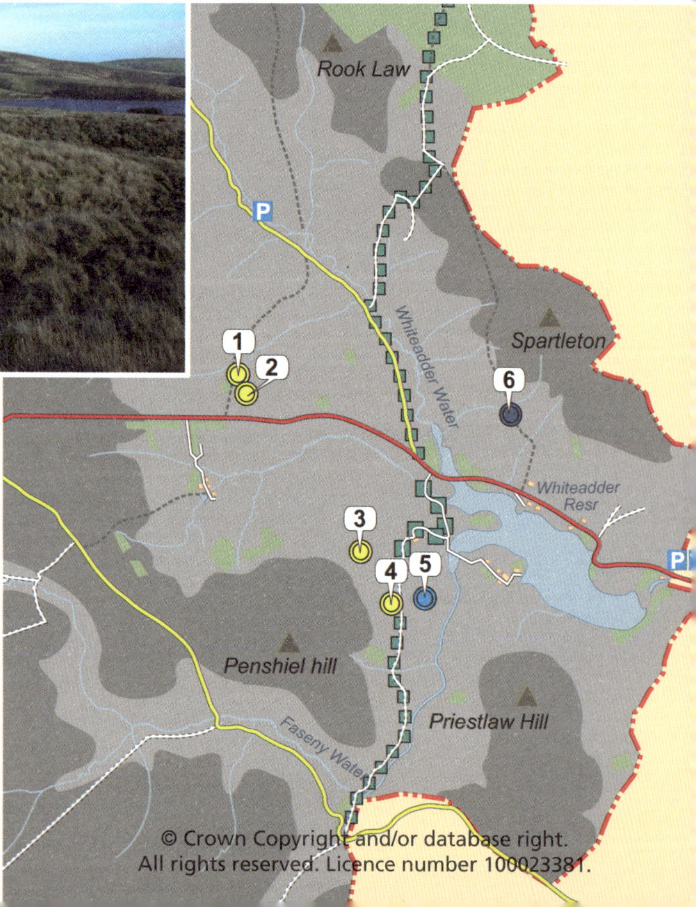

© Crown Copyright and/or database right. All rights reserved. Licence number 100023381.

1 KINGSIDE HILL STONE SETTING
Although relatively small in size, this *Bronze Age* cairn and circle of small boulders is thought to enclose a cremation cemetery. Take the path along the west side of the field. Please note that this field often contains stock, please keep dogs under proper control. There is restricted access during the shooting season.

2 KINGSIDE HILL CAIRNS
Two stone cairns are clearly visible in the field. Although some of the upper-most stones are probably clearance stones, the remains of two circular *Bronze Age* burial cairns are believed to survive beneath. Take the path along the west side of the field. Please note that this field often contains stock, please keep dogs under proper control. There is restricted access during the shooting season.

3 THE TABLE RINGS, PENSHIEL HILL
See opposite.

4 THE CHAPEL STONE, PENSHIEL
See left.

4 THE CHAPEL STONE, PENSHIEL (above)
A single small standing stone may be all that remains of a larger stone setting (such as a cairn or circle). Take the Herring road track south of Penshiel and the stone is opposite Penshiel *Grange*. Please note that this area often contains stock, please keep dogs under proper control. There is restricted access during the shooting season.

5 PENSHIEL GRANGE
The ruins of an extensive monastic *grange* can be found at Penshiel with traces of a tower and staircase, a courtyard, walls, and various buildings. The *grange* was attached to Melrose Abbey and although Penshiel is mentioned in a charter of 1200, the *grange* was probably built in the 15th century. Take the Herring road track past Penshiel for approximately 500m then cross the field to the *grange*. Please note that this field often contains stock, please keep dogs under proper control. There is restricted access during the shooting season.

6 GAMELSHIEL CASTLE
See opposite.

GLOSSARY

Aerial photography	Photography taken from the air (commonly an aeroplane, balloon etc)
Airship	A steerable self-propelled aircraft without wings, consisting of a large bag filled with gas which is lighter than air and driven by engines
Anglian (Angles)	A Germanic-speaking people who had settled in England
Anti-tank blocks	Lines of concrete blocks placed on the ground to impede tanks or armoured vehicles
Arquebus	A late medieval small firearm
British (Britons)	Native, indigenous population
Bronze Age	The period between 2000 and 800 BC
Burgher	The owner of land or a house within a burgh (town)
Buttress	An architectural structure built against or projecting from a wall which serves to support or reinforce the wall
Carmelite	A Roman Catholic order founded in the 12th century
Chancel	The area around the altar of a church for the clergy and choir
Cropmarks	Cropmarks appear due to the differential growth of vegetation over buried remains and can be seen and recorded from the air, especially during times of drought
Doocot	Dovecot or dove/pigeon house
Finial	An ornament at the top of a spire or gable
Friary	A building or community occupied by one of the four mendicant orders of friars or nuns (Augustinians, Carmelites, Dominicans, and Franciscans)
Glover	The open dome which frequently sits on top of doocots, allowing access for the birds
Goddodin	The post Roman indigenous tribe in the Lothians whose capital was Edinburgh
Grange	A monastic farm
Hill fort	An enclosed, defended settlement located on a prominent piece of ground
Hunter-gatherers	Pre-farming people who lived primarily before 4000 BC. They obtained food by hunting, fishing and gathering
Iron Age	The period between 800 BC and 400 AD

Jougs	A metal collar used for punishment and attached to a structure such as a church
Limekiln	A kiln used to reduce naturally occurring forms of limestone to slaked lime that could then be used in agriculture and building construction
Mercat	Market
Mort safe	An iron frame designed to protect the bodies of the dead from disturbance
Motte	An artificial mound topped with a wooden tower
Neolithic	The period between 4000 and 2000 BC
Pilgrimage	A long journey often to a shrine of importance to a person's beliefs and faith
Pre-industrial	Usually defined as before 1750 AD
Presbyterian	A number of different Christian churches adhering to the Calvinist theological tradition within Protestantism
Privateer	A person who owns a ship and has a licence from the ruler of a country to attack the ships of other countries
Promontory fort	An Iron Age settlement often found on the coast or close to a river which utilises nearby natural features (such as cliffs) as part of the defences
Reformation	A religious movement of the 16th century that began as an attempt to reform the Roman Catholic Church and resulted in the creation of Protestant churches
Rough Wooing	The period between 1544 to 1551 when England was trying to form an alliance with Scotland through the forced marriage of Mary, Queen of Scots, and Edward, the English Prince of Wales, son of Henry VIII. On Henry's behalf, the 'Protector Somerset' (the Earl of Hertford) invaded Scotland in 1544
Saltire	The Scottish flag
Saltpan	An industrial complex where sea water is accumulated and evaporated to make salt
Skewputt	A block of stone set at the top of a wall to finish a parapet, coping or gable
Votadini	A pre Roman indigenous tribe in the Lothians whose capital was Traprain Law

Scottish Outdoor Access Code

Know the Code before you go

Enjoy Scotland's outdoors. It's a great place that contributes to your quality of life, your health and your awareness and enjoyment of your surroundings. Everyone has the right to be on most land and inland water for recreation, education and for going from place to place providing they act responsibly. These rights and responsibilities are explained in the Scottish Outdoor Access Code.

Know your access rights

Access rights cover many activities, including for example:

- informal activities, such as picnicking, photography and sightseeing;
- active pursuits, including walking, cycling, riding, canoeing and wild camping;
- taking part in recreational and educational events;
- simply going from one place to another.

These access rights don't apply to any kind of motorised activity (unless for disabled access) or to hunting, shooting or fishing.

Access rights can be exercised over most of Scotland, from urban parks and path networks to our hills and forests, and from farmland and field margins to our beaches, lochs and rivers. However, access rights don't apply everywhere, such as in buildings or their immediate surroundings, or in houses or their gardens, or most land in which crops are growing.

KNOW THE CODE BEFORE YOU GO
SCOTTISH OUTDOOR ACCESS CODE outdooraccess-scotland.com

Know the Code...

Access rights come with responsibilities which are fully explained in the Scottish Outdoor Access Code, though the main thing is to **use common sense**. You need to **take responsibility for your own actions, respect the interests of others and care for the environment – what does all this mean?**

When you're in the outdoors, you need to:

- **Take responsibility for your own actions** – The outdoors is a great place to enjoy but it's also a working environment and has many natural hazards. Make sure you are aware of these and act safely, follow any reasonable advice and respect the needs of other people enjoying or working in the outdoors.

- **Respect people's privacy and peace of mind** – Privacy is important for everyone. Avoid causing alarm to people, especially at night, by keeping a reasonable distance from houses and private gardens, or by using paths or tracks.

- **Help farmers, landowners and others to work safely and effectively** – Keep a safe distance from any work and watch for signs that tell you dangerous activities are being carried out, such as tree felling or crop spraying. You can also help by:

  - leaving gates as you find them;
  - not blocking or obstructing an entrance or track;
  - looking for alternative routes before entering a field containing animals;
  - not feeding animals;
  - using local advice so that you can take account of shooting and stalking;
  - not damaging fences or walls; and by
  - avoiding damage to crops by using paths and tracks, by using the margins of the field, or by going over ground that hasn't been planted.

- **Care for the environment** – Our environment contributes greatly to everyone's quality of life and health. It's important that you:

  - follow any reasonable advice and information;
  - take your litter home;

- treat places with care, leaving them as you find them;
- don't recklessly disturb or intentionally damage wildlife or historic places.

- **Keep your dog under proper control** – If you have a dog with you, it's very important that it doesn't worry livestock or alarm others. Don't let it into fields with calves or lambs, and keep it on a short lead or under close control when you're in a field with other animals. **If cattle react aggressively to your dog, let go of it immediately and take the safest route out of the field**. Take care to ensure that you or your dog don't disturb breeding birds. Pick up your dog's faeces if it defecates in any place where it is likely to cause concern to other people.

- **Take extra care if you are organising a group, an event or running a business** – Consult the full Code or our website for information about your responsibilities.

If you're a farmer, landowner or someone else managing the outdoors, you need to think about the needs of people enjoying the outdoors. You need to:

- **Respect access rights** – Access rights extend to most of Scotland so don't unreasonably obstruct people on your land or water. Only lock gates when it's essential for animal health or safety and don't put a fence across a path without putting in a gate to allow access. Providing paths and tracks is a good way of integrating access and land management.

KNOW THE CODE BEFORE YOU GO

SCOTTISH **OUTDOOR ACCESS** CODE **outdooraccess-scotland.com**

- **Act reasonably when asking people to avoid a particular area whilst you're working** – People respond best to polite and reasonable requests, so keep safety measures in place for the minimum time, tell people about alternative routes and explain why the original route shouldn't be used. Remove information that is not up to date.

- **Work with your local authority and other bodies to help integrate access and land management** - Showing people that they're welcome and working with your local authority, or your national park authority, and others will help you successfully manage access over your land and help care for the environment.

If you're responsible for places where access rights don't apply, such as a farmyard or land surrounding a building, respect rights of way and any customary access, and work with your local authority, or your national park authority, and others to help improve and manage access.

Find out more about your access rights and responsibilities – and also about rights of way and customary access – by picking up the Scottish Outdoor Access Code or visiting www.outdooraccess-scotland.com. If you are having access problems - get in touch with your local authority or national park authority (see your local phone book). If you would like to have a copy of the full Code phone Scottish Natural Heritage on 01738 444177 or email pubs@snh.gov.uk.

Look out for other approved guidance which carries the Access Code logo.

Statutory access rights were established by the Land Reform (Scotland) Act 2003 and the Scottish Outdoor Access Code was approved by the Scottish Parliament on 1 July 2004. The rights came into effect on 9 February 2005.

TRAVEL IN/AROUND EAST LOTHIAN

GENERAL

Traveline	www.travelinescotland.com 0871 200 22 33

RAIL

National Rail Enquiries	www.nationalrail.co.uk 08457 48 49 50
East Coast	www.eastcoast.co.uk
First ScotRail	www.scotrail.co.uk
Virgin Trains	www.virgintrains.co.uk

BUS

E&M Horsburgh	www.horsburghcoaches.com
Eve Coaches	www.eveinfo.co.uk
First UK Bus	www.firstgroup.com
Lothian Buses	www.lothianbuses.com
Perryman's Buses	www.perrymansbuses.co.uk

Details correct at time of going to print.
Please check with operator.